The Spirit of the

A creative Journey into the Soul of Mother Nature

Vernon Hutter

AUSTIN MACAULEY PUBLISHERS™
LONDON • CAMBRIDGE • NEW YORK • SHARJAH

A CIP catalogue record for this title is available from the British Library.

ISBN 9781035804184 (Paperback)
ISBN 9781035804191 (ePub e-book)

www.austinmacauley.com

First Published 2024
Austin Macauley Publishers Ltd®
1 Canada Square
Canary Wharf
London
E14 5AA

This book is dedicated to my beautiful daughter Jasmine...

For the hours, days, and weeks that we lost...

Look deep into nature, and then you will understand everything better.

~Albert Einstein

INTRODUCTION

CONNECTING OUTER NATURE TO INNER NATURE

As a child, I grew up on Exmoor in South West England, where the natural world was all around.

The sky and the sun was my father, the earth and the land were my mother, the moon and the oceans were my sisters, the trees were my brothers and the animals were all part of me.

For a period of time, I moved away to the city.

Not only did I feel detached from Mother Nature, but I felt detached from myself and my inner core.

I felt a 'knowing' within me that I would always return to my source, where I could feel 'whole' once more.

Being apart and separate from nature affected me in a physical, mental and spiritual way.

The human race is 'part-of' and not 'apart from' Nature and the Earth.

We rely on her for everything that we stand for, which is why it's so important to look after her.

This book is a restorative journey, expressed in photographs and creative words.

It conveys the process of regaining our true nature by reconnection with Mother Nature. There are four processes, in which I have travelled the journey from the beginning, and can be a guide for others to emulate...

Reflection, Reconnection, Strength and Growth and finally Change and Transition. The Creative Spirit is a the bridge to becoming connected to the Spirit of the Earth once more.

And when we have reconnected to Mother Nature, then we are able to heal our inner nature and fulfil our true purpose.

*And into the forest I go
To lose my mind
And find my soul*

~John Muir

Nature it's not matter only,
She is also spirit

*~**Carl Jung***

Reflection

Remembering what was, both positive and negative.
Meditation and contemplation in nature.

Remembering

Do you remember how you whispered to the stars at night, and felt hypnotised by the spirit of the moon?
Or did you?
Do you remember a time when there were no scars or wounds chasing you?
And time was something that didn't mean anything or matter too soon?
Or did it?
Do you remember how easy existence was,
And thoughts were just moments that floated in the sky, and everything just was?
Or was it?
Do you remember splashing through puddles and singing in the rain? because that's all you needed to do?
Do you remember when you belonged to the sunshiny fields, because the sunshiny fields were simply a part of you?
Because if you remember those golden and precious moments, then those times are with you to stay...
And the next time you see a sunset or a puddle, then you'll shamelessly know what to do

V. Hutter '21

Reflective Moments

Spend time reflecting on where you have been, and who you have been. But always remember that where you have been, and who you have been in the past, doesn't define who you are in the here and now, or where you're going in the future.

V. Hutter '20

Patterns

Many of us unconsciously replay past patterns.

Patterns from our own past behaviour, and even patterns that we have learned from parents and parental figures, from our pasts, and from their pasts.

Sometimes simply reflecting this to others, as well as ourselves, we are able to make new conscious choices.

Choices made in the present moment, with a totally fresh awareness...

V. Hutter '20

The Black Sheep

I haven't always felt that I've been the perfect citizen and conformed to society along the way.

But sometimes being a black sheep from the system has had its advantages.

It's giving me more freedom to think for myself, freedom to say no when I mean no and yes when I really want to.

Freedom to be more creative, creating the light in life that I want, not what society wants.

Being the black sheep has widened my frame of reference, seeing the whole picture and not always the picture that I'm supposed to see.

It's also given me the mind to challenge imperatives, such as 'should do's', 'must do's', 'ought to's'.

And given me a chance to look at the reframed alternatives, like 'could do's' and other possibilities. When I'm on my last legs in life, I'm going to say to myself:

"I'm glad I was a black sheep"

V. Hutter '20

Twilight Swimming

Twilight is the transition from light to dark and dark to light, it's neither one nor the other.
It's a strange place where nature is in limbo.

I love swimming and walking during this peculiar juncture.
For me it's a time to process why and how my life goes from light to dark and dark to light, and how to restore equilibrium.

V. Hutter '20

In a bright and sunny faraway
land, sat a black
and white troll with black
and white hands...

Reflections

The lockdown period has been a very strange time.
But it's been a chance for reflection.

Reflecting on how we've been as individuals, how our lives have been up to this point in time, and how the society's we live in, have been in the past, and currently are in the present.

So in turn, with this renewed realisation, we all have a chance for change, individually and as a society in general.

V. Hutter '20

Sunshine Swimming

Warm early Spring-like sunshine swimming in February...
We're finally seeing the light at the end of the tunnel.
So feeling warm, Spring-like sunshine on my skin is fantastic!

V. Hutter '20

Grey Days

There are many different shades of grey.

Sometimes looking for the colour on a grey day seems impossible.

I find that in challenging times, everything can look more cloudy and grey.

But grey is the transitional colour between black and white.

So when the days are darker and clouds are in the sky, staying present with the grey is all that is required.

The Sun will always shine through the clouds again, and the day will always overcome the darkness of the night.

All we're able to do ourselves, is to be the best version of ourselves, in the present moment, and under the present circumstances.

We are in a liminal space, an in between world. A place for acceptance and contemplation.

A place to re-evaluate, reinvent and re-establish the future. Find time to celebrate the in-between spaces.

Whether it's walking or dancing in the rain, swimming in the sea, watching the raindrops on the window sill, in the moment or something else completely.

... sunny days are never far away...

V. Hutter '20

The Shadow Self

Where there is light, there is also a shadow. The source of the light creates the shadow.

The sun casts a shadow over the dark side of the moon, it shapes the night from the day.

It influences the seasons and rhythms of the earth, and throws a shadow over the solar system and Mother Nature.

According to Jungian psychology, the personality also has a shadow side.

And it's the shadow archetype that projects unwanted or uncomfortable fractions of the personality onto other people.

But the shadow or unknown parts of the personality can be both positive as well as negative.

Therefore the potential that we're unaware of, lies within the shadow self.

This may be, or may never be discovered.

V. Hutter '20

Reconnection

Awareness of what is and
finding meaning of who
we are on the Earth.

The Me Today

We are nature and nature is us.
Nature belongs to no-one and yet we belong to nature.

Nature can also be a therapist, and it's a therapist that is free.
All we have to do is tap into it, reconnect to life and become part of
nature again.

Just by being mindful in nature we can begin to heal.
It's a very simple process, it's using what we have already—our senses.
Being aware of what is going on in nature, in the here and now, we become
present and by being present we begin to heal ourselves.

What can you smell?
What can you see?
What can you hear?
What can you feel? On your skin, in your heart, emotionally and spiritually?
And what can you taste?

Yesterday's Me has been and gone,
Tomorrow's Me is yet to be, but when I stop thinking and just be, The Me
today is all I need to be.

V. Hutter '20

For the Moment Anyway

Even on the darkest of days, the wild flowers of the Heather and Gorse can brighten the landscape.
The flowers also give off a wild musky aroma, and there's a gentle serenity in the breeze.

How do you find peace of mind in an ever-changing and uncertain world?

The rhythms of nature are certain.
The sun still rises, the moon still waxes and wanes, the seasons just are and the birds still migrate... for the moment anyway.

Sometimes there's no need to try, like the seasons, but just let everything be as it is.
Because that's how it's meant to be...for the moment anyway.

V. Hutter '20

The Here and Now

When you swim in cold water, it completely obliterates overthinking.
All you can focus on is your breath and moving to keep your blood
flowing.
In turn, you're completely in the present moment, the here and now.

V. Hutter '20

Find Your Flow

I find most of my answers when I'm connected to the Spirit of
Mother Earth.

Connected to the earth—beneath me,
Connected to the water—the sea,
Connected to the fire—the sun,
Connected to the air—all around me,
And connected to the spirit of nature flowing through me.

V. Hutter '20

Barefoot on the Earth

I feel at peace in the countryside, on the moorland, by the riverside and close to the sea.

On the mountain top, in the raindrops, underneath the stars and barefoot on the earth.

Within the woodlands, gazing at the moon, listening to the birds and watching the sunset.

So when my equilibrium gets shaken and my life becomes unsteady, I know where my peace is.
And a peaceful soul is a happy one.

V. Hutter '20

"In every walk with nature, One receives far more than he seeks."

John Muir

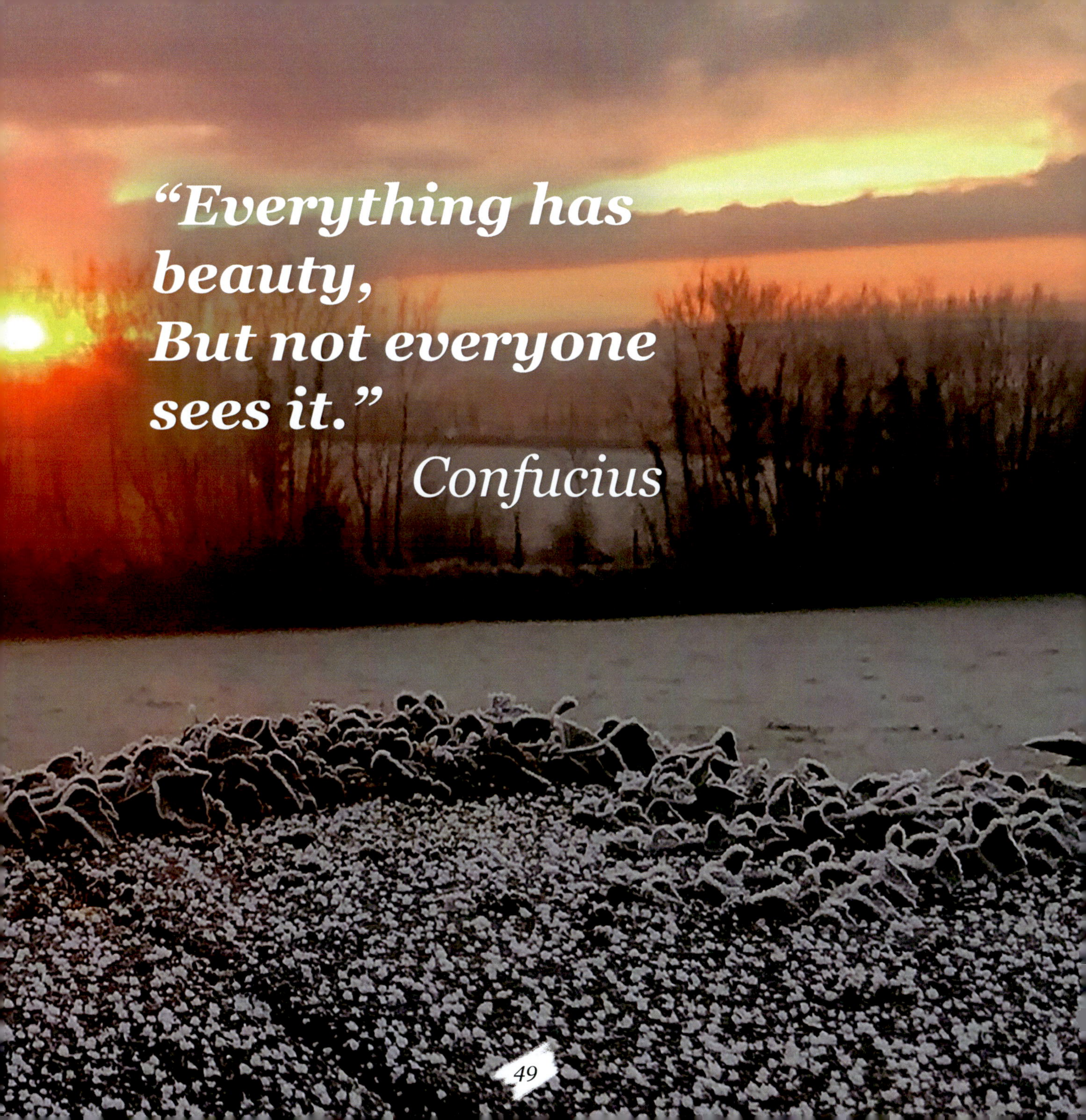

"Everything has beauty,
But not everyone sees it."

Confucius

Connecting and swimming
with the Irish Goddess of
the sea and Queen of the
Banshees
Chlíodhna...

Sometimes you just
need to walk to the
top of a hill...

Take a deep breath...

And let it go...

V. Hutter '21

The Rhythms of Nature

The Sun still sets in the evening and rises in the morning.

It's not aware of the establishment and man-made rules.

It's not aware of pandemics and rising mental health issues in mankind.

It's not aware of the massive divisions and prejudice that separates societies on the Earth.

The sun simply rises and sets, the moon simply waxes and wanes, birds carry on singing and the seasons don't change.

So when society is in turmoil and our man-made system is in chaos,
I find solace in Mother Nature, where everything just is as it is, and the rhythms just are as they are.

V. Hutter '20

Abandoned Lake

I love this lake at this time of year, it's very peaceful.

I can truly feel at one with the water;
The plants, the trees and the earth...
The air and the clouds;
The light of the sun and the Spirit of the Earth.

V. Hutter '20

Be still when in Mother Nature...

and Mother Nature will be still within you.

V. Hutter '20

Nature will always
nurture your inner
sunshine, if you
nurture mother
nature herself.

V. Hutter '20

We Are Never Alone

Many of us feel isolated at times during our lives.

Along with isolation comes loneliness.

But I've seen a lot of people returning to their source within nature, to reconnect again.

Because we are never really alone when we are by ourselves. There is that one consciousness that connects all creatures, plants and elements in this world.

That one consciousness is called Mother Nature.

Look at the tiny things that she has given us, and the huge space. From the microscopic world, to the huge mammals that roam the earth.

From the clouds that float in the sky to the wonder of the stars and universe as we know it.

This is a time, a special time, humankind is waking up.

We are reconnecting and realising that she is both beautiful and far more powerful than the human race at the same time.

So when you feel alone, then step outside, take a deep breath, re-engage and rediscover this incredible life that we've been given.

V. Hutter '20

What do different outer landscapes tell us about different aspects of our inner landscapes?

This is Lands Ends in the UK, the furthest south-westerly point on the mainland.
It's a wild, free, untamed, uncultivated Celtic land with a rugged coastline.

Weather Front

When do you feel like you have to change your weather front?

My daughter once said to me that she has to be different, with different people in different situations—with teachers, friends and family for example.

I explained that it was completely normal and sometimes we have to be different in different situations.

We all have sub-personalities.

Sometimes we have to adapt our personalities in front of friends, family, in a work situation, when we are alone and in many other situations.

But when are we our true selves? The non-adapted and core self?

It's so important to be with our core self on our regular basis, so we know who we really are.

When are you the sunshine and when do you need to be?

When are you the rain? When are you stormy?

And when are you engulfed by the fog or project a dense fogginess?

When do you become the ice and when are you the snow?

When are you multi-dimensional like a rainbow?

Do you become a fierce wind or are you a gentle breeze?

Have you ever dried up and sizzled out like in a harsh drought?

V. Hutter '20

I Am the Wind

I am the wind
And I am the waves

I am the sky
And I am the sea

I am the light
And I am free...

I am the sand beneath your feet
And the sunshine upon your skin

I am your thoughts that blow in the breeze,
With the Spirit of the Earth and the Spirit of the Seas...

V. Hutter '20

Gratitude for Mother Earth

Mother's Day is a special day.

It's a day when we say thank you to all the mothers and mother figures in our life.
But Mother's Day is even more special than we think.
It is a Thank you day to everyone's mother—Mother Earth.

For giving us the beauty of all of nature, the land, the seas, the skies and the creatures that walk beside us in the journey we call life.

Like our own mothers, Mother Earth can be forgiving, when we do her wrong.
She feeds us when we're hungry, nurtures us when we are lonely.
She gives us peace when we need serenity.

Mother Earth gives us spaces and places to be happy and have fun.
When we feel oppressed, Mother Earth gives us freedom.
Mother Earth gives us inspiration, when we are blind to see a future.
She gives us warmth when we are cold, and cools us when our mood is getting warm.

Mother Earth even gives us love and holds us, when we need connection.
And when we are completely connected to Mother Earth, we are never alone.

So if you get a chance today, say thank you to all mothers and mother figures, but don't forget to say thank you to Mother Earth.

V. Hutter '20

The Rocks and Trees Are Your Emotions

Whenever you go outside, first of all see the visuals all around you.
And then, very slowly and gently...

Hear, smell, feel and be aware of your whole environment.
And in time, notice how your inner nature relates to outer nature, on a metaphoric level.

Look at the rocks and trees on a personal level, as if they are your emotions, because
they are.
They belong to you and you belong to them...

V. Hutter '20

Breathing with the Spirit of the Sea

The spirit of the sea is almighty, when you breathe alongside her immense power,
she is willing to blow away the unwanted intensities within your essence.
Not only does she whisper these away,
She also quietly restores, reanimates and resurrects something deep within your core.

When you have a perpetual connection and understanding of Mother Nature, she has a
profound compassion for your innermost self.

We are all in synergy with the Great Spirit of the Earth... When we open our eyes and see
her majestic beauty, breathe through her hair, listen to the beat of her heart and feel the
expression of her energy,
then the union of integrity returns within.

V. Hutter '20

And It Was All Yellow

Buttercup meadows

Whenever difficult times are close by, look to Mother Nature, because she will always illuminate the things that matter.

Have gratitude for what life is in the present moment, because the present moment is all we have...

The here and now.

V. Hutter '20

No-Where Yonder

There's an old trail that I once used to wander, that goes deep into the forest, on the middle of no-where yonder.

Where time forgot to go and the people no longer chatter, Whence yesterday is never-land and tomorrow's don't matter.

Except to become the forest as the forest becomes me. And I am the sky, I am the Earth,
I am the birds and the wind blowing free.

V. Hutter '20

The Kinship of the Earth

There is one thing that connects us all, in these disconnected times, that one thing is Mother Nature.

The Earth we stand upon is the same Earth that supports the trees and creatures of the world.

The sky we marvel under is the same sky that the birds sing and glide in. The trees and creatures of the planet exchange oxygen and carbon dioxide.

The moon that shines in the midnight sky, is the same moon that pulls the tides, and can even affect the behaviour of plants and creatures.

The plants and animals feed the plants and animals.
The rivers flow into the sea, and the seas connect the land.

The sea support the fish, the fish and creatures support each other. The forests create the rain and the rain sustain the forest and land.

The Sun that warms the Earth is the same Sun that gives life to all living creatures on the Earth.
We are all part of, and not separate to, something much bigger than ourselves—Mother Nature.

V. Hutter '20

Immersion

When I'm fully connected and immersed in the natural world,
everything looks different and becomes more vivid.
Everything feels possible and is more lucid, and all life becomes fully
alive and awake.
My senses become hyper-aware and I can reach the sky through the
trees again.

V. Hutter '20

Finding Balance

How are you finding your balance in today's sometimes unbalanced world?
I've been finding mine through walking and being in nature much as possible away from work.
But without Mother Nature, I'm not sure how I would find a balanced body, mind and soul.

How are you finding your balance?

V. Hutter '20

Strength
and Growth

Conscious confidence to
find new pathways and
become who we're meant
to be.

Cycles of Life

As the heather and gorse start to wane away, and go back into the earth, so many of nature's other cycles come and go.

Mother Earth has many cycles—the migration of birds, the lunar cycles, seasonal cycles, tidal cycles, hibernation cycles and so on.

Just as life in general has it's cycles, from being born through teenage years, middle age and old age to death.

So the point that I'm trying to make, and see around me every day, is that nothing is permanent—and that makes every day a gift. When someone gives you a gift, make the most of it, and make the most of each day.

V. Hutter '20

A Wider Frame of Reference...

There are many different perspectives in the present moment.
Moving forwards isn't always about looking forward, sometimes it's about looking all around and seeing a completely different and wider frame of reference.
This can be done with everything and anything in life.

Many people have their own views and opinions.
Unfortunately when opinions about other people are negative, they become prejudices.

To let go of prejudice is a positive act.
After all most prejudice is made up of archaic mindsets.

When we are at peace with others, we are at peace with ourselves.

V. Hutter '20

Sunshine after the Storm!

Whenever a storm comes, be present within it, even when it's uncomfortable.
Feel it and don't push it away, nothing is permanent.

The sun will always shine again and the storm will always pass.

V. Hutter '20

Autumn Whispers

There's a spirit on the moor that whispers in the cool Autumn air.

She whistles through the golden bracken and dances over the feather-like clouds.
Singing sweet songs that can throw sunshine over your heart and sprinkle sparkles
upon your crisp breath.

She is neither here, nor is she there and yet she is all around and everywhere.
She is alone and she is together, with everything...

The Earth, the Sun, the rivers and the air all around.

V. Hutter '20

A Speck in the World

Spend some time looking up today.
High winds and high trees.

Just by looking up, we can realise just how insignificant both ourselves and our problems really are.
We are only a speck in the world, our world is only a speck in our galaxy and our galaxy is only a speck in the universe...

Take a deep breath in...let go...smile...life includes everyone, everything and all of nature.

V. Hutter '20

The Wild Inside!

I'm very lucky to have Exmoor on my doorstep, a place where I grew up.
So for me it's easy to find the wild and free part of my soul.
But no matter where you live, whether it's a city, town or in the countryside,
our wild selves are always present.
And that's the key, to be present, and when we are present we are free.
It's ironic that the wild and free part of us, deep down and inside of us, is
silent, still and calm.
Can you find your wild inside?

V. Hutter '20

Dance of the Wild Stallion...

The easiest way to become interconnected to my true nature and be in alignment with the whole of nature itself, is to heal my inner nature.

To heal my inner nature, I need to go into nature alone for a period of time.

Synchronise Mother Earths Five elements—earth, air, water, fire, and spirit with my six senses—sight, hearing, touch, smell, taste and spirit.

Native Americans and the Celtic traditions have also been known to do this... this is given many names, including Vision Quests and Nature and Wilderness based Retreats.

Either way, this helps me to connect with something transpersonal, and in turn opens a vortex that connects me to my inner purpose and true nature. This then allows me to transcend the chaos whilst keeping my feet firmly on the ground.

By walking on a separate path to many others in society, may look quirky or even slightly insane.

But to walk in the same direction, would be to travel in the opposite direction from my true nature.

So dance like a wild stallion in a storm, swim like a dolphin on the crest of a wave, breathe like the wind rustling through the trees and love this life with the same passion as a spring flower reaching for the sky!

V. Hutter '20

Trees Are Our Family

Trees are so much like humans, only vibrating at a different frequency.

Like us, they can be thick skinned and yet delicate on the inside.

When they get knocked down, somehow they're able to grow again, and sometimes even stronger.

They have many branches, all going in different directions.

Trees often have strong roots, but these can also be vulnerable at times.

And they're able to weather a storm, despite being often exposed, during the worst of the winds.

Trees are our brothers and sisters, they're our mothers and fathers.

Trees are our family and friends.

V. Hutter '20

"Nature does not hurry,
Yet everything is
accomplished."

Lao Tzu

"The earth has music
for those who listen."
William Shakespeare

Inner Landscapes

Nature is a part of the individual...
We are all created from, exist in, and return to nature.
Each of nature's elements also exists within us—Earth, Water, Air, Fire and Ether or Spirit.

We are all of these elements and all of these elements are one with ourselves.

When we fully accept and integrate our inner landscapes then our outer landscapes also change.
Not only do these landscapes change but our whole understanding of the universe and existence change at the same time.
This state of being is also known as being synchronised with the Universe.

V. Hutter '20

Going into the woods
can be like taking a
journey deep into the
subconscious mind,
both light and dark and full of mysteries...

V. Hutter '20

Wild Rosebay Willowherb...
Nature always makes me feel
humbled and overwhelmed at
the same time.

The World Simply Is

When you take time to stop, look, hear, smell and feel the real world—you become truly alive.

In this space there is no room for worries, unhealthy thoughts or feelings.
You simply are and the world simply is.

When you reconnect to the true source, then no matter what life becomes, it will always be ok.

V. Hutter '20

Wisdom of a Tree

Trees have the most amazing ability to grow, flourish and bear fruit, all in the space of a year.
And when they need to, they are able to let go, quite freely. Trees have the capability to branch out into many directions... always looking for the sky and growing towards the light.

They're able to overcome a storm and have the capacity, to be flexible enough, to weather endless elements in their lifetime. Sometimes the breath of earth can knock them down.
But they still have an amazing determination to grow again, only in a different way and direction.

Trees are absolutely incredible creatures, we have so much to learn from them, because they are our relatives... they are a part of us, as much as we are a part of them.
So the next time you see a tree, be aware that it knows that you are there, as much as you know that the tree is there.

And if you need a hug, then most trees will gladly welcome you. Whenever you're going through a struggle, and can't see anything but fog in front,
ask yourself 'What would a tree do when it loses sight of the beauty ahead?'

V. Hutter '20

Look to the sky...
When in doubt, look up.
There are signs within the clouds and there are directions within
the stars.
Nature always holds the answers.

V. Hutter

Sing Out Loud Again

If the wind wildly blew away your sorrows and swept up your pain,
as the sun willingly shone upon your heart, so you could sing out loud again...

If the bees caught your worries, and flew them into a land that smells of sweet honey,
Whilst the sun and the moon shook hands, as the shimmering light became no more...

If the sea washed off the fears that you were never to see, and the clouds rained away your
tears when you lay down on this earth...

How would it feel, to be who you're meant to be?

V. Hutter '20

When I need to be high or
intoxicated, I go high in
altitude and find the sheer
beauty of nature
intoxicating.

V. Hutter '20

Change
and
Transition

Metamorphosis, Redefining
a New Journey.
A knowing of who we are
and are meant to be.

Seeds of Intention

When you plant a seed, It will either grow or it won't.

So when you plant the seed of hope, or seeds of future intentions, they'll either grow or they won't...

The most important thing is that you've planted the seed in the first place.

V. Hutter '20

Stand Tall

When the yesterday's have flown away and the tomorrow's are far to be,
We have a magical moment in time, and then it's gone, So breathe and set your
fearlessness free...

Never chase what's behind you, because behind is never there,
Sing and fly with this moment, as it shines through your soul, that whistles through the air.

And when you catch a glimpse of what there is to be,
Say thankyou as it floats away.
Walk forward, breathe and let it go, with your feet on the earth, on this special day.

So stand tall as you are, a magnificent creation on this earth, We are not the past and we
are not the future,
And every sunrise shines a new birth.

V. Hutter '20

Pain Is a Seed

Going through trauma can be very painful.
But the pain is a seed.
If the seed or pain is nurtured, then it's able to germinate...

We all experience pain at some point during life.
When the pain is accepted and not buried too deep, it becomes a seed.

And if that seed is given the right conditions, then it can grow into something special.

V. Hutter '20

Motherland

This is my homeland.

Moorland, vast spaciousness and wild countryside.

It is my landscape.

My inner landscape feels a deep connection to the Earth here.

When I am away from this land, I sometimes feel fractured.

It runs deep within my veins and is part of my soul.

I am related to every part of this wonderful wild and free land. I sense a metaphoric and interrelated, kinship to Mother Nature all around.

The fallen tree, has been battered in a storm and knocked over.

But it has resilient determination and is still grounded.

It simply grows and flourishes in a different direction, because it's journey wasn't meant to be straightforward.

And in that way, it can show other trees that it can not only be rooted after trauma, but shine brighter than before.

V. Hutter '20

***

The stone in the photos is called the Caractacus Stone.

It has its current name after a descendent of King Caractacus, who led a resistance against the Romans 2000 years ago.

But there are many Neolithic burial mounds within several metres of the stone, therefore suggesting it is linked to that period.

There is a legend that a local Carter tried to dig for gold, that was thought to be buried underneath the stone.

The stone crushed him to death, and now the ghost of the Carter haunts the area.

Polarities...

Mother Nature consists of opposing forces and elements ... the Yin and the Yang, Night and Day, the Sun and the Moon, Summer and Winter;
Destruction and Creation, the Calm and the Storm, Birth and Death, Fire and Water and many others.

Sometimes people come to me and explain how hard they've been working at something, but despite their best efforts, they're still receiving negative feedback.
But without the negative and the positive together, ideas might never come into fruition.

So the next time you feel that you are experiencing a lot of negativity, despite your best positive efforts,
remember, it's because your ideas Exist!
... and without both the positive and the negative together, they can never fully materialise and come into complete creation.

V. Hutter '20

Grow Our Own Wings

I came across a Green Emperor Moth Caterpillar (Saturnia pavonia) on my walk this evening.

At some point it will catalyse and go through the process of metamorphosis.
In other words, it will continue to grow after birth, completely change, grow wings and develop into one of nature's wonders.

When we're born, we can follow our 'life script' and continue to crawl, like the caterpillar for the rest of our lives.
Or we can find our inner catalyst, discover who we really are, go through metamorphosis and grow our own wings.

V. Hutter '20

Dancing with the rhythms of the Earth...
When we dance with the rhythms of the Earth, life becomes effortless.
When life is effortless, inner peace sets us free from the imperatives that
can fog our direction.

No effort is needed to find who we are.
Who we really are, isn't found from years of searching externally. It is
inside waiting to be opened, when our inner nature is synchronised with
our outer nature.

V. Hutter '20

"**Adopt the pace of nature:**
Her secret is patience."
Ralph Waldo Emerson

"Allow natures peace to flow
into you, as sunshine flows
into trees."

John Muir

Our true direction in life
isn't always the obvious,
sunniest or even easiest one.
Be true to your authentic
self...

V. Hutter '20

Time to Fly

We are all creative beings, finding the key is part of the journey.

We are all parts of the sun and the moon, the clouds and the sky,

We dance on the earth and we sing to the sea,

But when we become the journey, then we'll be able to fly.

V. Hutter '20

Waves of Change

When black and white days with black and white waves,
Are transformed into a reflective silence, of a black and white haze,

When empty and nothing vessels, become alive with something specials,
Then the bellowing waves of smiling cheers, are born from the shivers of aching pain
and freezing fears.

V. Hutter '20

Land of Colour

Beyond the clouds of the Can't Do's,
Mustn't Do's,
Shouldn't Do's
and didn't Ought to's...
Lies a land of colour and sunshine, with the Can Do's,
Would Do's,
Will Do's and the
Being the things we've always Thought To's...

V. Hutter '20

Trees and Humans Are the Same Family

How thick is your skin?
Do your roots keep you steady?
Are your branches strong?
How upright and proud do you stand?
Do your branches go in many directions?
Are you flexible when a storm comes?
And when the sunshine is here, how does it feel?

Trees and humans are much more alike than we think, just vibrating at a different level.

V. Hutter '20

The Liminal Place

It's the liminal time again, with liminal possibilities and liminal dreams.

There are liminal futures beyond the liminal space.

And liminal horizons outside of this liminal place.

V. Hutter '20

"Nature is not a
place to visit.
It's home."
Gary Snyder

"In the wild breath of nature,
Feel the hush of presence."
Angie Weiland-Crosby

The Trees in the Forest

What's your relationship with the natural world?

What do you love?
What are you afraid of? What gives you peace?
What do you like and don't like?

Too often mankind looks at nature as something to be conquered.
Whether it's a mountain, the trees in the forest, the animals and fish from the land and the seas, or something else.

If only mankind would look at all of these things as something to be connected to, instead of conquering them.

What would it be like to be outdoors much more in all of the seasons? And therefore keeping our connection with nature all the year round?

Walking in the hills, bathing in the forest, swimming in the waters or dancing in the rain.

Open up your whole being to Mother Nature, guided by the spirit of the universe.

V. Hutter '20

The Passing Space

There is something very mystical about the time when the light and the dark overlap.
In this transitional time of day I quite often swim or walk outdoors.

It's a time when I feel close to a different realm of reality, almost like two
dimensions colliding.

It's the Twilight and Other-Worldly time, when a spiritual haze is present and the
bird song has been engulfed by a liminal and transcendental silence.

V. Hutter '20

New Beginnings

Can you see the Phoenix?

The Phoenix represents eternity and foreverness.

It continuously goes through transformation.
It also represents death, endings, rebirth and new beginnings.

So the analogy of the Phoenix rising from the fire can be very powerful, especially at times where circumstances have come to an end and existence is no longer what it was.

This form of symbolism can be powerful at different times of life, when endings make way for new light.

It's the rebirth, restoration, regeneration and emerging from what was, with renewed youth and energy.

V. Hutter '20

The Place where Space forgot Time...

Being present in the moment, is timeless and transforming

It's a place where time forgot space and space forgot time,

It's a supernatural expanse where anything can materialise,

A place where legends and the little people can exist,

A crossing-over and transpersonal magnitude, where the small things in life are the most precious.

V. Hutter '20

Our Ball of Energy

We wake up with a ball of limited energy every morning.

This energy can be used in either a light or dark way.

Which can be expressed through actions, words and thoughts.

So when you do kind and positive actions, speak and think well to yourself and others, then not only does your energy become brighter but so does that of others.

Remember to try and think, do and talk kindness, even in what can be sometimes an unkind world.

Shine and be free.

V. Hutter '20

One way to free up your inner nature and mental clutter, is to find space within Mother Nature.

And we all need the feeling of freedom, within what sometimes can be a restricted world...

V. Hutter '20

Jasmine

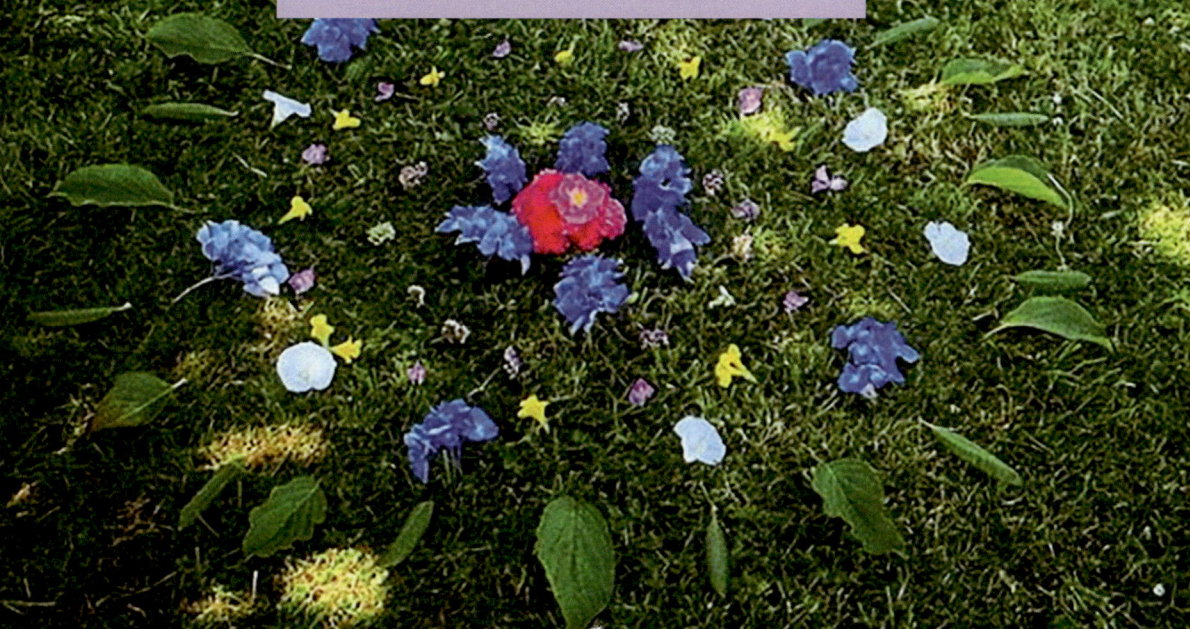

Thoughts can be both
good and bad and are
like clouds in the sky,

they come and then they go.

Jasmine Hutter '21

The colours in the sky reflect the colour in my life...

Jasmine Hutter '21

Candlelight burning
bright,
Countryside open
wide,
Happy as can be,
In the fresh air and
feeling free.

The night is mysterious
The sky is beautiful
This moment is special
And my mind is relaxing...

Jasmine Hutter '21

A Brief Word about Vernon and Jasmine

~~~~~~~~~~~~~~~~~~~~~~~~~~~~~~~~~~~~~

Vernon is a qualified psychotherapeutic counsellor and nature-based therapist. He has counselled adults and young people in various settings, including HMP Exeter.

Vernon has worked as an Ecotherapist on Dartmoor in the UK, and is currently the founder of Wild-Spirit Well-Being, a nature-based therapeutic company on Exmoor in the UK. Jasmine is a bright happy-go-lucky teenager, also living in the south-west of the UK.

She is creative, vibrant and extremely self-aware, with a very positive and outgoing attitude to life.

Several years ago, they were both separated as father and daughter due to a breakdown in a relationship.

But despite the period of time between seeing each other, there is still an incredible father-daughter bond.

Acknowledgements.

~~~~~~~~~~~~~~~~~~~~~~~~~~~~~~~~~~~~~~

All photographs and words by Vernon Hutter, except pages 173-179, where the photographs and words are by Jasmine Hutter.

Silhouette model, page 103 – Jasmine Hutter.

All editing and design are by Vernon Hutter 2022 with the support and help of Joanne Hutter 2022.

Wild-Spirit
WellBeing, Ltd.

www.wildspiritwellbeing.com

Spirit of the Earth
A Creative Journey into the Soul of Mother Nature

~~~~~~

The human race is 'part-of' and not 'apart from' Nature and the Earth.

We rely on her for everything that we stand for, which is why it's so important to look after her.

This book is a restorative journey, expressed in photographs and creative words.

It conveys the process of regaining our true nature by reconnection with Mother Nature.

There are four processes, in which I have travelled the journey from the beginning, and can be a guide for others to emulate... Reflection, Reconnection, Strength and Growth and finally Change and Transition.

The Creative Spirit is a the bridge to becoming connected to the Spirit of the Earth once more.

And when we have reconnected to Mother Nature, then we are able to heal our inner nature and fulfil our true purpose.

V. Hutter '21

www.wildspiritwellbeing.com

~~~~~~~~~~~~~~~~~~~~~~~~~~~~~~~~~~~~~